Mid life ramblings of a menopausal mum

Melanie Walters

Mid life ramblings of a menopausal mum ©
2022 Melanie Walters

Presentation by *BookLeaf Publishing*

Web: www.bookleafpub.com

E-mail: info@bookleafpub.com

ISBN: 9789357615150

First edition 2022

To my mum: thanks for your inexhaustible supply of love, advice and unintentional material for this project. I love you x

To my children: I hope this inspires you to step outside of your comfort zone now and again to do something a bit crazy- you are my world, you both amaze me and I adore you xx

To my long suffering husband: After 26 years of marriage menopause dictates that some days I like you and some days I don't, but I will always love you xxx

ACKNOWLEDGEMENT

To all those within the inner circle of my life, whether you know it or not there are probably snippets of our interactions in these pages ... I thank you all for inadvertently contributing.

My Turn

As a mum, I've reached the age where I find
myself exasperated,
The family just drive me nuts, expletives
whispered & x-rated.
So now I find the only way to gain some civil
conversation
is try the last remaining choice....the cat; to gain
some validation.
Someone sees me, someone cares, although even
he has airs and graces,
He needs to fed, and a nice warm bed, (usually
mine)
'Coz cats don't do personal spaces.
With that in mind dear reader, I would give you
some advice..
When young love blossoms within your soul,
your head and heart agree "he's nice"
Before you know what's happened, you're a
wife; and then a mother.
The first child keeps you sleep deprived, and
then you find you have another.
The house, the car, the daily grind, all drive you
to despair,
You blinked and now the house is full of teenage
angst and devil may care.

I've been told it comes full circle. That I'll miss
them when they fly the nest,
But right now the only thought I have is "When
is it my turn for a rest?"

Turkey for one

Turkey for one
Is not much fun
So don't let them be on their own,
If you are able:
Find room at your table
No one should spend it alone.

Christmas should be
The presents, the tree
The trinkets, the food, and the wine.
But more than that,
It's the giving of something
That money can't buy;
It's your time.

The fun
and the games,
The quality street
Christmas's pudding, Buck's Fizz, a mince pie,
With no one to share it
It isn't the same
An emotional void-
A sit down and cry.

It's tears for the family

No longer here,
For the husband
Or wife passed away.
It's beans on toast
Can't be bothered to roast
Just because it is Christmas Day.

So wrap them a gift,
Pull up a chair,
It's not so hard to do;
It's a "two for one" gift, to show them you care:
It also gives something to you.
It will fill up your heart,
With a feeling of warmth,
A purpose, a reason for living,
To know that you gave them
The most precious gift
And the best part of that - is the giving .

Ode to a cat

5

Oh to be a cat,
How I would like that
I could snooze all day , and be happy and fat.
I could sharpen my claws,
And paddle my paws
On a chair, or a sofa, or cushion, or lap.
One pitiful meow
Is how
I'd get them dancing to my tune,
I could stay out all night
Enjoy the odd fight
Then stroll in and snooze until noon.
oh to be a cat,
 Yes .. I think I would like that.

New kid on the block

 We moved house a few years back
(Because the school looked better here).
This area was well sought after,
The beach and woodland walks were near.

Moving day passed without a hitch,
Its a day I will remember,
We just had to crack the "new school" thing,
the first week of September.

Uniform bought,
new bag, pens, and books,
Off we went, both feeling fraught,
exchanging nervous looks.
"I'm a little bit scared mum- Ive got butterflies
in my tummy"
"let me tell you a secret son- so have I; isn't that
funny!"

"I'm sure when you come home today,
you will have made friends, and had a great
time"
 I nod, and smile , and encourage him in..
"go on- you'll be just fine"

At 9am the bell rang,
the children lined up straight away,
with waves and smiles to mums and dads,
cries of "bye love -have a great day".

I look around the sea of faces,
none of which I know,
I need to make new friends now too,
No idea which way to go .

A group of women smile at me
and two of them come near
fancy coming for a coffee?"
 We see that you are new here!
With relief I smile back,
"yes please if you don't mind;
 Im feeling a little nervous,
Thats really very kind".

So off we go-and as we chat;
the time flies by, so much so,
that after booking play dates in,
We collect the kids from school.
And out he comes with a great big grin
" hey mum - this is my new friend - he's cool"

So the new school nerves weren't needed
It was all just in the mind,
It turns out that actually it seems:

most people know to just be kind.
Make those new faces welcome,
Include them in your fun,
When making plans; ask them along
In case you're ever " the new one ".

The delinquent OAP

Now I'm old and grey ,
I'm not gonna behave,
It's not the best use of my time.
Now I'm old and grey-not working all day;
The time I have left is all mine.

I could walk in the park,
And feed bread to ducks
But I don't think that sounds quite "me"
So I think I should find some mischief, some
fun,
With a glass of wine - or three.

Share jokes with friends,
And laugh too loud,
To keep them all on their toes,
When I'm in a mixed crowd
just what I will say-no one knows.

Yes, I think that would make my day
Don't think I'll be quiet at parties ,
"Home early to bed?" This old lady said
"I want to be dancing right till the end-
I can catch up on sleep when I'm dead".

The Tradie wife lament

When your partner of choice is a tradesman,
It's a life not like another,
There's a constant stream of their "tradie" mates-
but they all step in and help each other.
When disaster strikes or things go wrong:
at the drop of a hat, they're there…
they make a mess, drink gallons of tea,
their jokes hang blue in the air.
To get it done; they work til late
its a private members club,
"No payment needed mate-
Just buy me a pint in the pub"

A tradiewife has a funny old life,
She exists in a DIY limbo.
There's always a little unfinished bit,
 With the odd dodgy tap, or that drawer; all
akimbo.
 Be it bricky, sparkie, chippy or plumber
 They all seem to act the same way,
" I will do this for now-It works just fine"
With a smile and a wink they say.
"If it won't open, just give it a whack,
right there- that sweet spot at the back"

But when all's said and done
I think that my life
Is alright, and I'm glad
that I'm a tradiewife.

Teenage boys bedroom

Why do boys bedrooms smell so bad?
their bed, their clothes, their shoes,
Its like something has died in there,
Im gonna have to go in; search for clues.

What on earth is that fousty stench?
its rancid, rank, and rotten,
could it be the the football boots ?
or the half eaten sandwich; long forgotten?

I vacuum, clean and launder,
Make it all look neat,
but still it lingers; the boys just say
"don't worry mum, its bit of bum, and bit of
feet".

Wordsworth Im not

I don't wander lonely, as a cloud,
But I do wonder, and ponder, and mutter out
loud.
When my mind is unsettled
My thoughts and ideas,
Become words written down, until the fog
clears.
The overloading effect of my life on my brain
Is a cause for anxiety, worry and strain
But a pencil, or pen with a notepad that's new
Can turn it around; unveiling the view.
The worries then flow down my arm to my
hand,
Like a puzzle revealed, ,I then understand
And though no great poet, I enjoy a rhyme
And the rhythm of words like a beat; keeping
time.
So William Wordsworth, Dylan Thomas and
Keats
Can sleep well, relax, They can all rest in peace.
No prizes are likely that's not why I write
These poems just help me to sleep well at night .

Skinny jeans

Middle age spread,it has to be said,
is really quite a pain,
Try as I might, my jeans are too tight;
The zippers broke again

My bras don't fit me anymore
They either ride up or dig in,
I remember when it wasn't
such a challenge to be thin.

The blouses all gape at the front,
The buttons have all popped,
The dresses daren't be "bodycon"
The jumpers no longer "cropped".

I run to keep fit; but no luck there,
The scales are not my friend.
Stubbornly pointing ever upward,
When will this dieting nightmare end?

Just a couple of pounds is all I ask,
I just want to weigh a bit less,
But I have to admit as I get older,
It's harder and harder to have success...

So Instead I look for wide leg pants,
And jumpers that are "slouch"
Who needs nights out in skinny jeans?
I'm happier sitting on the couch.

Mans best friend

A most loyal companion
He waits by the mat,
For the man to pick up the lead.
Don his coat and his hat,
Grab his door key, and glasses,
And the walking stick that he needs.
Off out the door
Tail wagging, eyes wide
Nose twitching,
Can't wait to get sniffing outside.
Chase the ball, find a stick,
Or Maybe a puddle,
Then back home in the warm,
Give the old man a cuddle.
Fetch him his slippers,
Fall asleep on the mat,
Man will not find a friend better than that .
He doesn't have family
Just a four legged friend,
Who won't leave his side
Loyal right till the end.

Hindsight

When I was younger, I worried..
About how I looked and what I said.
My knees were knobbly, my arms too long,
I wished my curly hair; straight instead.

Hated the sound of my own voice.
Awkward making new friends,
Often said the wrong thing,
With no clue how to make amends.

If I could give myself some good advice:
It would be to not worry about all that.
'Coz when I see photos of how I was then
(even tho' I had thought I looked fat).

I was tall and slender,
Fresh faced and bright eyed,
I Didn't see the beauty of youth,
Or the enthusiasm inside.

But now that I am getting old,
and I like to think I'm wise,
The wrinkles don't really bother me,
Neither do my wobbly thighs.

My body is a wonder; It's got me to the big 5-0.
And if I look after it, who knows
How much further I could go ?

Hindsight is amazing!
The power to look back and realise
It doesn't matter if you're fat or thin,
We are not validated by our size!

What matters it we seize the day;
The little moments we can treasure.
Live life for the here and now,
'Coz we won't be here forever.

The M word

Sometimes I get crabby, It's really quite absurd,
My husband says I'm stabby, All it takes is one
wrong word..
To cause a row, upset the mood Or have me long
for solitude.
It's not my fault -I can't control these mood
swings up and down,
Try as I might ,I'm quite a fright, I just can't
hide it when I'm down.

I'd like to say I find it funny when the red mist
has receded.
But in reality: I don't, There's just one thing
that's needed.
A bar of chocolate helps, and then retreat into
my quiet place,
Pour myself a glass of wine, Insist my husband
gives me space.

He can cook the dinner..The kids can wash the
pots,
I know it doesn't seem like it..But I love them
lots-like jelly tots.
I feel that I don't know myself. But at least I
know the cause,

I've reached that dreaded time of life...
The blasted menopause.

Teenage summer

The smell of the sea
Factor 15
Beach bar-b-ques
99 ice cream.
Surf in the sun
Salty hair
Tanning young skin
And freckles on fair.
Boys in lonch shorts
splashing around
bikini clad girls
drawing hearts in the sand.
Drinks in the sun
Then fading light
Dancing and fun
Into the night.
The summer goes fast
The tans start to fade
Loves young dream
Memories Evade.
Like the ebbing tide
Upon the shore
The sun sinks away
And its winter once more.

Footie mum

It's an early morning roll call.."C'mon get into
the car!
Got your shinpads?... and your boots?
No! you cannot wear them in the car."
Arriving at the pitch side, the kids all rearing to
go,
The mums look less enthusiastic (its ok - only 90
minutes to go).
Wrapped up warm against the cold, and
sideways beating rain,
Armed with a warm cup of tea to hold, and sip
now and again.
Praying for no injuries today; can't have more
time off school,
I'm hoping he gets picked to play, (I'm
struggling with the offside rule).
Huddling up with other mums, encouraging
words yelled out,
Trying so hard to enjoy it; but freezing from all
the standing about.
Then suddenly its over and a victory's been had.
The kids all come back tired;but smiling... so I
guess it's not that bad.

Adulting

I don't want to be grown up any more,
I am tired, and everything aches
Can I go back to being a child again please?
Maybe, aged 5, 6,7 or 8.

Those days were such fun in the summer,
Never short of fun stuff to do,
Water fights, camp outs and days on the beach
Or garden sprinklers to run through.

Christmas looked forward to with anticipation,
Leaving Santa some milk and mince pies,
Looking forward to the next days celebration,
Waking up, excited, but with tired eyes.

Games in the street with the neighbours kids,
Jump the rope being spun in a loop,
Riding bikes fast, stopping with a skid
Finding out who can do hula hoop.

All of these things were taken for granted,
No worry or care in the world to be had.
But now I'm an adult, with husband and kids;
And I'm not saying all that is bad,

But I think that they say childhood is the best time;
And I have to admit I agree:
'Coz I find myself stuck in this cycle of mine
Laundry...housework, ...and " mum what's for tea?"

School run

There goes Anna, running late-A trail of kids
behind her,
Sally's lost her Meg again; The troops all rally to
find her.
There's gym bunnies in Lycra, Career mums
who drop n go,
Earth mothers swapping recipes with everyone
they know.

The ones who always arrive 'en mass' anxious to
set off;
The minute that the bell rings; they're off to the
coffee shop.
The tired mum who is 8 months gone, looking
for a place to sit
The single dad who looks harassed, his son has
forgotten his kit.

The one who brings her dogs with her and let's
them run around;
Scaring all the kids to death-It's chaos in the
playground.
I stand and watch the drama that unfolds in front
of me,
Then walk back home to peace and quiet....
And a nice hot cup of tea.

Flying solo

You think you know me,
I think- you think you own me,
But I don't wanna be with you
I think I'd rather be lonely.

You think you rule me,
Like to think- you fool me,
But I know that I'd be better:
Without you I'd be free.

There would be no-one to answer to
No war of words to battle through,
And no I dont really have any place to go
But I dont care - Im done - Im flying solo.

The unhappy runner

"You never see a happy runner"
That's what people say
"They all seem like they're in such pain;
why do they look that way."?

I must confess, I thought that too
But then gave it a try,
My legs were lead, my chest on fire,
I felt like I could cry.
But slowly over time that changed;
The legs no longer sore,
I managed to hit the 5k mark,
And then reached 5k more.

I may look from the outside,
like the running causes pain.
But I'm smiling on the inside,
And it helps to keep me sane.
Doesn't matter that I'm not the best,
I don't care that I'm slow,
What matters is I'm doing it,
Don't care how far I go.
The endorphins that engulf me,
As I get on with my day,
Is the reason I get out there,

To run, and look that way.

So if you see a runner -
Who looks like they might just die,
Or you think" what makes them do it?"
It's that amazing " runners high" ! ●

Hairdressers chair

The hairdressers chair - a confessional box,
A place to talk and share.
There is no consequences here,
Just understanding care.
A space to get things off your chest,
And feel you're listened to,
An oasis of indulgence,
No matter what you're going through.

I think what makes them think aloud,
And talk so candidly,
Is their own face staring back at them,
inner thoughts that they can see.
It's like they're talking to themselves,
So no one else can hear,
That piece of glass reflecting,
As their mind begins to clear.
They relax whilst being primped and preened,
Secrets Shining from their eyes,
The gossip or the crisis,
That the mirror won't disguise.

It sees them with their guard down,
All defences fall away,
As they relax, and sit, and chat,

Not quite knowing what they say.
It seems to spill without control,
The rivers bank a-burst,
Those tentative embarrassed tears,
An apology at first,
But then they seem to relish it,
Gradually unwind,
A chance to get things off their chest,
To share what's on their mind.

" I would like it to look different,
But still like me" they say.
So as I pick up the scissors,
And begin to snip away-
There's transformation In their mood,
I see them now uplifted,
Thankful for the ego boost,
To them that I have gifted.

Girls weekend

Im going on a girls weekend, let me explain
how we begin....
Bottomless brunch to start us off-with cocktails
all thrown in,
A bacon bap or fry up, With toast (
posh-sourdough)
Scrambled eggs cooked to perfection,
Or poached on avocado.

Then a mooch around the town, to nose in all the
shops
When we're ready for a break; it's a scheduled
coffee stop.
Find out what there is see, what fun stuff we can
do
Check out the local markets, Have another drink
or two.
Now - "where to for the evening?"- looking for
a slap up meal,
"Oh look! a cosy local pub, with home cooked
food- ideal."

Doesn't matter what we're doing really,
 the company is the key
Coz these weekends away with friends

Are what makes me feel like me,
Not mum, not daughter, Nor a wife
No labels for a while
I can just be myself again
And that's what makes me smile.

Frenemies

You know how sometimes; You think you've got
a mate,
Someone you can confide in and trust,
Then it turns out you were wrong, they dont
care,
They're not there, They're not fussed.

So keep your friends close, but your enemies
closer
Behind your back: doing things they're not
supposed to
Keep your friend circle tight, But hold your
enemies tighter,
Then that dog that you thought a companion;
can't bite ya.

Frenemies, are a dangerous breed,
If you see what they're doing,
Dig them out; like a weed,
They're leeching; feeding on the best parts of
your life,
Just waiting for the chance to stick in the knife.

They're not for me, I don't need 'em
A "friend" like that is no mate..

A line crossed, thats a sign,
It's not friendship - it's hate.
That hate is a waste of my effort and time,
So just "do one mate"
You are no friend of mine.